Peace
WITH
Broken Pieces

Donte' Richards

Copyright © 2021 **Donte' Richards**

All rights reserved. In accordance with the U.S. Copyright Act of 1976. Scanning, uploading, copying and/or electronic sharing of any part of this book without the permission of the author is unlawful piracy which is considered theft of the author's intellectual property. No part of this book may be reproduced or transmitted in any form, whether electronic or mechanical, including photocopying, recording or by any information storage or retrieval system without written permission from the author.

Communicate with Donte' Richards
www.donterichardsenterprise.com

ISBN-Paperback Edition: 978-1-956184-03-7

Printed in the United States of America

Published by Abundant Life Publications LLC
www.abundantlp1.com

PEACE WITH BROKEN PIECES

Acknowledgements

I take this time to acknowledge my fiancé Stephanie, for always being there and believing in all my dreams.

To my children, I haven't always been present because of the choices I made in life, but just know, I'm ready and I love you!

To my uncle Marlon, but more like my brother, you are and always have been my mentor and guide Bro. Your knowledge, wisdom and energy are unmatched. So, just for you and me, let's play chess.

To my sisters, Toy-Toy and Brit-Brit; to my little brother, Aaron; I love you more than you could ever know. Although I am the oldest, because of past choices I was not there to assume that role, yet and still you've loved me unconditionally.

Last but certainly not least, I want to give big love to RCA (St. Charles) for starting me on my journey to the life that God put me here to live. To my RCA family, but now lifelong brothers: Walt, Scott, Anthony, Pastor Bill, Micheal, Coach Dave, Chris, Dan and Joey, we fight the good fight every day. This one is for us brothers!

Let's Heal!

PEACE WITH BROKEN PIECES

Dedication

I dedicate this book to my loving mother,

Melody "The Captain" Richards.

I am thankful for your unconditional love and support,

for always putting your children first

and the many sacrifices you made for everyone.

I just want to say, "This one is for you."

I love and miss you so much mom!

I dedicate this book to my dad,

Ronald "Ronnie Red" Richards.

Until I see you again Mom and Dad,

I will make you proud!

Donnie

Table of Contents

PEACE WITH BROKEN PIECES

Introduction
Pre-Game Pep Talk: Page 10

Pre-Game Warm-Up: Page 12

First Quarter: Page 16

Second Quarter: Page 28

Half-Time: Page 38

Third Quarter: Page 42

Fourth Quarter: Page 58

Overtime: Page 84

Post-Game: Page 90

INTRODUCTION

Pre-Game Pep Talk

I've thought for over 20 years,

wow, my life would make a great book.

But the thought alone,

wasn't enough to fuel me to write the book.

PEACE WITH BROKEN PIECES

I've also thought,

I could write a book and make a lot of money.

But that also wasn't a reason good enough to write a book.

Now, finally, as I sit in rehab at the age of 45, broken, humbled and at my absolute rock bottom, I've finally found a reason that is more than enough to tell my story, expose my life to the world, expose the depths of my failures, yet also my journey towards spiritual peace and joy. Ironically, the reason has less to do with me, and more to do with helping the many people out there, like me. I'm telling this all too familiar story, so that so many others will read my story, the story of this once broken man that has risen and know they too have a place and a purpose on this earth. I want you to know that you are great, and you are visible, because I see you!

I want you to know that it's okay to not be okay.

Through this book, "Let's Heal Together!"

Pre-Game

WARM-UP

As I began this journey of telling my story, what amazed me most was how much I didn't know myself.

Remember, this is my story, my life, so I'm supposed to easily know how this story should be told, right? Wrong. When you've spent as many years as I have pretending, disguising, and creating my own false reality, sitting down to put my story on paper was extremely difficult, extremely hurtful and extremely humbling. But I moved forward in telling my story because this is the only way to achieve what I like to call, "Extreme Healing."

First Quarter

PEACE WITH BROKEN PIECES

I was born in Gary, Indiana November 14, 1975. On that day I can only begin to imagine what was going through the mind of my teenage mother. The excitement and love, yet so much fear and uncertainty.

All the questions that must have been going through her mind: "Can I do this? How will I do this? Am I enough? How much is enough? Is 'my enough' sufficient for this innocent, fragile, vulnerable and dependent little boy?" Now that I've gone through life; many times, choosing to run from so many things, I've truly gained a whole new level of respect for the woman who forged ahead. She did whatever needed to be done and sacrificed whatever she needed to sacrifice for my greater good! Amazing! So, here we are, a teenage mom with her new baby boy, ready to take on the world. Fortunately, we are both blessed with Virginia "The General" Underwood.

Before I go any further, allow me to explain the titles I gave these two strong and resilient women. In my later years, I began to refer to my mom as "The Captain." She was our leader, the glue to everything for everyone. Mom was the staple that you could count on no matter what was needed. Spiritually, mentally, financially, no matter what it was, mom would never let you down.

Big Ma (Virginia Underwood) was "The General." She was the reason why my mom had that "by any means personality" when it came to taking care of the family. They were two truly special women. Okay, so that's the origin of the titles given by me to my mom and my grandmother. For the first years of my life, my mom and I lived with Big Ma. Big Ma's door and home was always open for her children. Her loving and nurturing nature has been and will always be that blanket for all her children and grandchildren.

PEACE WITH BROKEN PIECES

Later in the pinnacle of my addiction, unkept and definitely living my worst life; each time Big Ma would see me, she would pull me in the house with pure love and feed me. She made sure I was in a safe space, even if only for a moment. "The General's Love" was unconditional, I love my Big Ma.

My mom and I lived at Big Ma's house with my uncles and my auntie. My early childhood years were blessed and fun. However, I watched my mother scratch and claw for everything she achieved, all while being "enough" for me. She finished high school, then worked at McDonald's all while putting herself through college. She was definitely a "warrior." Now, I know what you're thinking; you've said so much about your mother, what about your father?

This isn't a "Pity Party."
This is a "Healing Party."

Timeout

PEACE WITH BROKEN PIECES

I had to take a timeout before telling you about my father. This topic was confusing to me in my earlier years and a crutch for me during my later years, as well as in my addiction. See, I was cursed with being the oldest. Now, my sisters and brothers will tell you that I was our mom's favorite and yes, I must say, I was definitely spoiled.

My mother and the decisions that she made, showed me what it looked like for a woman to always put her children first. But the curse of being the oldest is powerful! I understood what was going on. I felt and understood that something wasn't right, and those memories followed me, untreated for forty plus years. If I had to sum up "the curse of being the oldest" in two words, they would be, "I REMEMBER."

My eyes saw things that should not have been seen by a child. My ears heard things that should not have been heard by a child. And most importantly, my unconscious mind was being molded on what a man should or should not be. It was developing narratives and creating false realities about how to treat a woman, when, where and how to show emotions and so much more.

As I recover and heal, I am extremely careful with how much blame I lay on my father. I now accept responsibility for my part, my arrogance and my choices that led me to my "Rock Bottom."

Let's Heal!

Resume

First Quarter

My father was born Ronald Lemonte Richards in Boston, Massachusetts. But to everyone and I mean everyone, he was best known as "Ronnie Red." Now, my father and mother hooking up gives true confirmation to the cliché that opposites attract. My recollections of my father during my early childhood are distorted. As a result, all I have are validated stories, told by others, about my dad.

He was a young man, growing up in Gary, Indiana, lost in the world of gangs and violence. He ran with some of the toughest cats around and he definitely held his own as it relates to the street life. With all that being said, I ask, "Where does that leave a baby boy that's clinging to his mother's bosom; and not yet aware of how much he needs the male presence of his dad?"

After many years of blaming my dad for not being all I needed him to be, I've grown to understand that although he had issues, he loved me. I traveled through life blaming him and being arrogant about what I deserved. I constantly used the excuse of not having his true presence as to the reason why I was as I was in each area of my life. Then I was given a rude awakening.

That awakening did not come from reading a book. That awakening did not come through sessions with a therapist. That awakening came from the most effective teacher, "experience." God said to me, "I'm going to allow you to live your father's exact life." Everything I didn't like about my dad, I unconsciously became. I was irresponsible. I was not a clean and sober dad. I was not there when my family needed me and that became my new normal. Through my lack of stability, I sabotaged all my relationships during that phase of my life.

That all led me to living an unfulfilled life. Talk about being humbled to the core. I now realize, my dad did indeed love me the best way he knew how to love me. He was by nature, a loving person. It was the addiction, which I came to know oh so well, that led him to be as he was and not his true self.

My dad unfortunately, was not able to overcome the addiction. He was tragically shot and killed in the midst of his addiction. But here I sit dad and I want you to know, I forgive you and love you with all my heart. And just know, I'm taking you along with me on this journey to lifelong joy. Until I see you again Dad, I'm going to make you proud!

Love you Dad.

Let's Heal!

Second Quarter

PEACE WITH BROKEN PIECES

I love it here! Our first house. The new neighborhood was called the "Miller Moats." My young parents went through the apartment phase in my first eleven years and now we were in our first home. It was small, but it was a house and it was our house. That is the neighborhood where I met lifelong friends: Jamie, Coleman, Big Lonnie, Brian, Tony, Vick(R.I.P.), Maurice and an entire neighborhood that became my extended family.

We all got along, played every sport together, did plenty of mischievous dirt together, but we always had mad love for each other. It was definitely a good time in my young life. My mom worked her way through school, then she worked as a substitute teacher. The one memory I have of her stint as a substitute teacher was during the time that I attended Nobel Elementary School.

PEACE WITH BROKEN PIECES

There I was sitting in class acting a fool with my friends. The door opened and my mom walked into the classroom. You can only imagine the look on my face as she settled in at her desk. I proceeded to raise my hand and ask a question. I made the mistake of starting that question saying, "Mom, instead of Mrs. Richards!" She quickly and firmly corrected her baby boy. And that was my mom, firm but always fair and with love.

During this quarter, our family seemed stable, but I truly believe that the blessing of being too young to truly know and fully understand everything that was going on, was temporarily protecting my innocence.

Timeout

The "innocence" of a child should always be protected by the parents with their lives. It is important to remember that nothing should penetrate the fortress that parents put up around their children. Our issues, life's evil deeds, evil places, people and things; nothing should get past the gatekeepers (the parents). This is the sacred, unsaid fact that is violated much too often.

As a result, you had a child exposed to grown-up situations. Why should I see mom in a domestic dispute? Why should I be exposed to the addiction that my dad was killing himself with and at the same time creating a chaotic environment? He was my dad, my idol. My level of confusion continuously increased, but that confusion quickly turned to anger. I learned anger early in my life. I was also infested with the false narrative that men shouldn't show emotions.

I rode an unhealthy "emotional roller coaster." And as you can guess, those learned behaviors followed me into my adult years. My beautiful, innocent children were also exposed to similar behavior. Sometimes it was the exact behavior that I witnessed as a child.

Yes, I failed as a father, but this isn't a "Pity Party." This is a "Healing Party." So, I say this, "As long as you have breath in your body it's not too late and for that, I give thanks to my Higher Power!"

Play Resumes

PEACE WITH BROKEN PIECES

So, here we are, going through life as a family. Not perfect, but nothing in life is perfect. There are now two children. I now have a little sister, Latoya, but we called her Toy-Toy. As life went on, my mother held it all together, while continuing to progress in life and keeping her dream alive of becoming a full-time teacher. Not just any teacher, but a teacher who cared; a teacher who believed that through consistent love, every child could make it and live a successful life.

One day mom and I took off in the car and she pulled up to a beautiful brick home. We got out of the car, went into the house and there stood a white gentleman. Turns out, he was the owner of the house and my mom was looking to purchase it from him. It was beautiful and I would have my own room. It was definitely an upgrade and I was excited! The neighborhood was called Aetna.

I wanted to live there, but it hadn't crossed my mind that in order to live there, I had to leave all my friends from the "Miller Moats." Forget that; they were my family. We eventually were blessed with the house, but it was bittersweet.

Yes, I could see all my boys at school and we still played organized sports together. Nevertheless, it wasn't the same as being able to wake up first thing in the morning to go outside and play or to play street football way past the streetlights coming on outside. But I guess it was time for me to enter a new phase of my life as a child. That transition shaped my life in so many ways. Identifying and now sharing it with the world has meant everything to my recovery.

Let's Heal!

"SURRENDER

WITH

NO

REGRET."

Perhaps that move was the beginning of me
learning how to practice a strategy
that I have named,
"SURRENDER WITH NO REGRET."

Half Time

So, let me get into the importance of true identity and identifying the role that it plays in all our lives. Yes, even the "normal people." The definition of identity is sameness of essential character, individuality, and the fact of being what is supposed. This word identity is, in my opinion, one of the most important words in our English Dictionary. Us succeeding in life, and functioning, balances on us truly understanding and embracing this word, identity.

In my opinion, when something is identified, it is understood. It has a "face," it has its own character, strengths and flaws. Each and every one of us was born and immediately given an identity. A name by our parents, a birth certificate by the hospital and a social security number by the government. All those things combined, form our identity and leads me to explain how the word identity was everything in my 26 years of failing at life.

PEACE WITH BROKEN PIECES

I've caused a lot of pain, suffering and struggle in my life, because of the choices I made. After doing a thorough and honest inventory of myself and my life, I truly believe I found the root of it all. I lost my identity. I had stuffed all my pain, suffering, exposure to violence, trauma, childhood experiences and grief so deep inside of me, that it all lost its identity.

From 19 years old until 45 years old I went through 26 years of acting out, wearing countless masks and not being who God created me to be. Instead, I was totally confused, frustrated, misguided and angry. I did not like how I was living my life. I didn't know how to fix it because I had no clue about what needed to be fixed. I just knew I hated who I was at that stage of my life!

All the while, all the things that lost its identity sat at the bottom of my soul and festered. And my identity wasn't the only thing I lost.

My existence was also lost for those 26 turbulent years! It was not until I addressed my alcohol and drug addiction, along with all the underlying issues and pain I had concreted inside, that I was able to start to get my identity back and truly begin to know the real Donte'.

To everyone reading this book, I encourage you to understand that you don't have to allow pain, grief, or any other issues to cause you to lose your identity. Deal with it and/or get help for it while it still has an identity. If you lose what it is, you lose you.

Let's Heal!

Third Quarter

PEACE WITH BROKEN PIECES

As our lives transitioned into our new home and neighborhood I held on to my old memories and friends. I began to make new friends in Aetna: Bernard, Fat Lie, Berry, Boogie, Keon, Myron and Fish, just to name a few. I also learned pretty quick that Aetna looked the part of a peaceful neighborhood with nice homes, but it was rough! We had a Skating Rink, which some people called, "The Rink" and some people called it, "Screaming Wheels."

Although it was right by our neighborhood, it seemed like everybody in Gary and even Chicago went to Screaming Wheels on Friday and Saturday nights. But with all the different hoods that came to "The Rink" it was apparent that Aetna ran the show there. Okay, back to it. I can't tell you how I met my first friends Myron and Mouse, but chances are that it had something to do with basketball. Aetna is where I fell in love with basketball.

PEACE WITH BROKEN PIECES

Yes, I had played in my old neighborhood, but that was in the streets with cut out milk crates attached to the light pole. Over here, basketball was played on real courts. Over here, some kids even had courts in their backyards and driveways. To me that seemed like what I call, "True Luxuries!" I began to play night and day. My mother would have to call me in every night because I was hypnotized by basketball.

As I write this book and my mind reflects, I now know the reason why I was so into the game of basketball. When I played, it took me away and made me forget everything. Point blank. Playing basketball made me forget everything that I did not want to remember or face that was happening in the world around me. Whether I was at practice, in a game or just playing basketball with my boys at their house or at the legendary games held behind Aetna Elementary School; I felt free! I felt empowered!

PEACE WITH BROKEN PIECES

I felt in control whenever I had the opportunity to play basketball! I felt unconditional love from the basketball. I bounced it and it always returned to my hand. When I passed the basketball, it went where I wanted it to go. When I shot it, no matter if I made it or not, I always felt through my intentions, which were always to make every shot, the basketball always felt what I felt. That bond between me and the basketball was an unbreakable bond.

As I said earlier, there were many things I should not have seen or heard and unfortunately, I was old enough to remember. My personality, demeanor and habits were molded by those memories and experiences that followed me for years.

Timeout

PEACE WITH BROKEN PIECES

Before going to rehab and continued therapy, I consistently blamed my dad for everything. Yes, he loved us, but he was still absent most of the time. Yes, when he was present, he cooked, cleaned, and made sure we were safe, but he still never attended any of my games during my formative childhood years. Yes, it appeared that everyone loved my dad because of his big heart, protective personality and sense of humor, but he was still very violent and aggressive.

All the "buts" are what led me to have so much resentment towards my dad. Ironically, all my dad's "buts" became my "buts" in my adult years. Through surrendering to a Higher Power, going to rehab, continued therapy and meetings, I was able to finally put away my arrogance and the judgment of my dad who is now deceased.

I now choose to heal, for the both of us. I choose to take care of my family as a man should, for the both of us. I choose to do the right thing, for the both of us. I choose to live a legacy focused life, for the both of us. I have learned that I have absolutely no right to judge anyone. As I point that powerful pointer finger at someone else, there are always three hypocritical fingers pointing back at me!

Let's Heal!

"SURRENDER WITH NO REGRET."

"Surrendering to do your work, as it relates to internal healing, can lead to the ability to stop external blame games."

Resume Third Quarter

PEACE WITH BROKEN PIECES

When I look back to reflect on my childhood now, I can see why I spent so much time at Big Ma's house. It was because as the oldest I knew, I understood and therefore my mom wanted to protect me as much as she could. That was my mother, she always put her children first. I loved being at Big Ma's house.

It was always fun because my uncle Marlon was there. But as I said earlier, we were more like brothers. Marlon was only a year and a half older than me. That's right. My grandmother had children before my mother, at the same time as my mother and even after my mother. That explains why I have an auntie named Angel who is the same age as me and an auntie named Tina, who is five years younger than me. Big Ma didn't mess around.

She gave birth to ten children and took care of each and every child with everything she had in her soul. I enjoyed going to Big Ma's house because everything was in order at her house. We played at her house and we ate good meals. There was no chaos at her house. Every morning I looked forward to the smell of sausage, eggs, bacon or the meal of her choice. The towels were laid out every morning for each child to wash their face before going to the table for breakfast.

She really instilled the principle of cleanliness being next to godliness. Lunch was set daily at 12:00p.m. Then dinner was set daily at 4:00p.m. Her house represented security in my life. Being at her house protected my innocence in life. Time at her house represented stability for me because I knew what to expect each time. Her ability to schedule helped me learn about the importance of structure in life.

All my family gathered at her house. If it was tragedy, joy or just because, Big Ma's house was the gathering place. One of my uncles was murdered and Big Ma's house was the gathering place after that happened. I was about twelve years old at that time.

Some of my long-term memories are affected by Post-Acute Withdrawal Syndrome, also known as P.A.W.S. However, I am very aware of what happened the night that my uncle was murdered. He came to our house and when he left, he was murdered.

I remember seeing the handprint of my uncle in blood because he had been left where he was shot. That was my first experience seeing tragedy up close and personal, but it was not my last. I was hurt and it turned into anger. I stuffed the hurt inside and kept moving through life. There was no therapy for me at that time.

PEACE WITH BROKEN PIECES

Now every day that I wake up, it is literally like a new life begins for me because I saw death at such an early age in my life. While I was riding my bike with the friends that I met in Aetna it was previously fun and games. After my uncle was murdered, I started noticing the high levels of violence that existed in our community. I had previously been shielded from violence by my mother, "The Captain" and Big Ma, "The General."

It was like hate began to take residence in my heart as a result of my uncle being murdered. It became easy for me to hate after that experience because my uncle was a cool uncle. As a twelve-year-old boy, I definitely looked up to him as an adult who cared for me. No matter what happened outside the house, I loved being at Big Ma's house because I got to spend a lot of time with my brother.

PEACE WITH BROKEN PIECES

We did just about everything together, but what I really enjoyed was when Marlon and I would go play basketball at the legendary Washington Park. Once again, basketball carried me through the confusion. I would be in a zone while on the basketball court. Therefore, all the loud music, rolling dice and drugs being sold had no effect on me while I was on that court. It was just me, the basketball and the rim, working in harmony to escape the chaos and life.

As we grew older, Marlon and I remained close throughout high school. He was always very protective of me and still is to this day. We still refer to each other as brothers and that will never change. Throughout my high school years, basketball of course, carried me through. Yes, I was a good student. Yes, I had a social life and made friends easily at school. Spud, John and Vincent were my closest friends.

However, I was still living with an emptiness, a longing to have that father and son relationship with my dad. When I look back, I wanted and needed that more than anything. That dad who would guide me and who would provide security. I wanted my dad to be in the stands at my basketball games with my mom.

I wanted to hear my dad say, "I'm proud of you son." I believe men reading this can relate. We were young men lost without our fathers. We desired to have guidance in our lives. My mom was the most magnificent woman ever to grace the earth, but with all the unconditional love she was able to give me, with all the sacrifices she made for me over my entire life, she was not able to truly teach a boy how to be a man.

Let's Heal!

"PRAY FOR YOUR PART."

Every person has an important purpose to fulfill on earth. I encourage you to invest the time to
"PRAY FOR YOUR PART."

Fourth Quarter

PEACE WITH BROKEN PIECES

I was ready to live my dreams and play basketball at the college level. I was well educated because my mother did not play about the importance of education. However, I settled for mediocrity in my study habits.

College was a very social time for me. I often told people that I majored in basketball and partying, while I minored in Communications and Business Administration. I was a hard worker as it related to basketball and any time that I chose to focus my mind to accomplish any task.

I moved to Dubuque, Iowa and it was a real culture shift. There was a population of 99% white people and a population of 1% black people. The day that I was being dropped off to attend college there was an active segregation rally taking place.

PEACE WITH BROKEN PIECES

Coming from a predominantly black neighborhood, my main interactions in the past with white people included playing basketball and the house that my mother purchased. I had never been exposed to racism. The rally was led by people who supported racial segregation. It was shocking to me that an event like that was happening in plain sight, on a main street at a Post Office in the center of the city. Witnessing the rally in person introduced me to the broken piece of confusion, while at college. It appeared that the confusion I thought I was escaping had found me at college. However, nothing could have stopped me from attending college because playing college basketball was my dream.

My mother cried and pleaded with me not to stay at college because of the rally. She looked at me and said, "Donnie No." I faced another broken piece labeled racism as I entered a new city and state to attend college.

PEACE WITH BROKEN PIECES

I could not turn back because I did not want to return to the broken pieces from my childhood. My mother was fully aware of the truth and the danger of the situation, but my mind could not be changed. What I saw in Gary, Indiana versus what I saw on television about college was two different worlds. I created my own reality and attending college represented better opportunities.

The move from the hood to the college dorm was a huge transition in my life. I am not sure if people really understand the culture shift that takes place in the mind of high school graduates that attend college in predominantly white neighborhoods, but it was a transformative experience for me. I had to learn a new way to be aware of my surroundings fast, just to stay alive. My mother gave me $100 and helped me unpack. All the while, the look on her face was anguish and concern.

PEACE WITH BROKEN PIECES

What I realize now is that she was very concerned about me, and she was right. She gave me three hugs. As a seventeen-year-old male from the hood, I did my best to reassure my mother that I was okay. However, I was in for a rude awakening because there were even more broken pieces at college. I was not okay and I had to learn how to be okay with not being okay.

My mother gave birth to me when she was seventeen years old. My transition to college at seventeen years old represented another form of birth and my opportunity to step into manhood.

As my mother drove off in our tan 98 Oldsmobile, I was ready to find a good party. After meeting my roommate and the people on the basketball team, I reflected on the fact that I had arrived in the world that I had dreamed about as a child. I was thankful that my dream had become my new reality, but I missed my mother and my neighborhood.

PEACE WITH BROKEN PIECES

The community surrounding the college did not accurately resemble my dream. My college experience was extremely different from my childhood. It was very different for me looking over my shoulder in the hood, than it was looking over my shoulder while attending college in a predominantly white neighborhood.

I was angered and confused by racism. Those were natural responses because I had already experienced being angry and confused from the challenges that I faced with my father. I often asked, "Why did people who were total strangers choose to scream racial slurs at me?"

One day while I was going to get ice cream at a gas station, there were racial slurs yelled out the window and it was very confusing to me. One student who was with me had been attending the college for one year and two students had been attending the college for two years. Everyone had a look of confusion during the encounter.

It was like we were in a dangerous cycle of racial slurs being yelled at us, followed by seeing the people who were yelling, experiencing the anger, then fighting. There was an internal fight because of the consistent racism on campus, but I did not have anything to return to in my hometown. Returning home would have represented failure for me, so I stayed at college.

I did not understand the significance of the rally that I saw on my first day in a new place, so I stayed. I had looked forward to the moment for so long based on the movies that I watched about college. Attending college also represented an opportunity to take the steps to break a generational curse. I didn't understand the depth of the generational curse, but I fully understood that going to college symbolized validation for me. I often said, "See, I can be different from my dad." When I was about eleven years old, I made it my mission not to be like my dad.

PEACE WITH BROKEN PIECES

I did not want to treat women how he treated my mother. He was a complex man, there was good and bad. There were days that he had the best personality in the world. There were also days when I was confused by the rejection that I received from my father. I didn't receive praise or validation from my father.

My substitute for validation and love was my love of basketball. Even in college, when I bounced the basketball, it came back to my hands. When I was between those lines it was nothing but love, pats on the back from my teammates and cheers from the crowd. College basketball with my name on poster boards and a special section at the game for me was life changing. The cheers from the crowd signified love for me. It was a combination of intoxicating and liberating, to have a personal cheering section for me at the basketball games.

PEACE WITH BROKEN PIECES

The validation that I didn't get from my father at home felt good to receive for my performance on the basketball court. However, the time after the basketball game ended was a time of isolation for me. I was lost and I often wondered, "Now what?"

While I was in college, my father attended my game for the first time ever. However, he was murdered three weeks later. My uncle called and told me that my father had been murdered because my mother could not tell me. I waited until the night before the family visitation to return to Gary from Iowa.

I placed my head on the casket and said, "We could have saved him." I have made peace with that broken piece. In reality, he was his own person. I had done enough as a son by getting good grades in high school, excelling at basketball, excelling in college and doing the best that I could to make him proud.

PEACE WITH BROKEN PIECES

When he died, I no longer had anyone to prove anything to in my life. In reality, my dream had turned into a nightmare. Life was so confusing because I had gotten into legal trouble due to drugs. I still played basketball and that trumped everything.

I was physically there, but not mentally present. My mind kept flashing back to the last and only game that my father attended. My dad was the first person to introduce me to basketball. He gave me my first basketball hoop when I was five years old. After his death, in my mind, every game that I played was the game he had attended. It was like I was not able to move forward.

One day I had gotten drunk enough and high enough from marijuana; the same feeling that I went to bed with, I woke up with the next morning. The term sleep it off usually means that you can go to sleep and wake up feeling better. Well, that didn't happen for me one night.

The next day I made a life altering decision to move. I was still living on campus in a basketball dorm at that time. I packed my bags as my two roommates sat in disbelief and watched me pack.

I was determined not to go back to Gary, Indiana to face the broken pieces in my past. I chose to stay in Iowa, but I drifted into a lifestyle filled with aggressive behaviors. Drugs and alcohol became front and center in my life. I hurt people mentally and physically. I once believed that hurt people, hurt people. That was until I gained a new perspective about the healing process.

Let's Heal!

Timeout

During rehab I learned about the healing process. As a result, I now believe that hurt people who take the time to heal will do all they can, to no longer hurt people. That is where I am in my life today. I go above and beyond to avoid intentionally hurting people.

When I was hurting I did not want to admit that I was hurt. I watched how some of the male figures in my life behaved. It was common for men to behave badly, but I did not always see immediate consequences for the negative behaviors.

From childhood through college, I wanted to be loved and shown that I was cared for by the people in my life. Now I realize that maybe their capacity to love was negatively affected by what they experienced or witnessed in life.

Resume

Fourth Quarter

PEACE WITH BROKEN PIECES

The complexities of grief and trauma that I experienced, led me to withdraw from college. I thought it was a major accomplishment to attend college for three years, from 1993 until 1996. Then in 1996, about eight or nine months after my father was shot and killed in 1995, more broken pieces surfaced. That is when my real life gave me another rude awakening.

Of course, I had contemplated leaving college previously; because what I experienced in real life, did not look like the dream that I had of college. My dream did not include racism, struggle, anger, or any of the challenges that I faced on the college campus and the community surrounding the college. I was worrying myself into oblivion about my mother and the challenges that she was facing at home without me. The year 1996 was the end of college life for me and the beginning of a downward spiral.

PEACE WITH BROKEN PIECES

I experienced more broken pieces on my journey. The embarrassment, disappointment, shame, and heartbreak became too familiar. I had made the decision to leave what I loved, basketball. It was a difficult decision because basketball was consistent in my life, even when it felt like the world around me was unstable. The patterns of anger turned into grief. Instead of properly processing the grief, I turned to seeking attention from women. Then life hit and the reality of two children being born led me to being so emotionless that I was not present for them.

I did not understand at the time that, but I was treating my children the same way my dad treated me during my childhood. I told myself that I was not worthy of being a father because I had just left what I knew and loved. It is important to invest the time in life to get to the root of negative patterns related to generational curses.

PEACE WITH BROKEN PIECES

When I experienced being emotionless, I believe it was a result of receiving whippings and being told that I better not cry. In my mind, as a young, African American male, I believe that added to the broken piece that I labeled confusion. The childhood experiences that caused me to be emotionless, also carried over into my life as an adult, father, drug addict and led to me being homeless.

When my children were born, I did not consider myself a responsible father. I visited, but I felt unworthy, like I might mess up something for my children. I felt unworthy to provide my children what I did not see provided for me by my father. The children represented me all over again. I was running from college, running from my responsibilities, running from reality and running into the unknown. I worked a series of odd jobs, but it was not enough to sustain an adult life. I was extremely irresponsible during that phase of my life.

PEACE WITH BROKEN PIECES

I only worked the job long enough to get a check. The jobs that paid every two weeks did not work well for me because it was like I had to work three weeks for one check. When I quit basketball, all the structure that existed in my life was gone. Being responsible seemed strange to me. I was hopeless, lost, confused and emotionless. That state of mind did not serve me well. The drugs assisted me with numbing myself.

Any time that I was not high, I was always in search of getting high again. It was damaging to my body, mind, soul and spirit. Using crack cocaine was like a graduation from marijuana. It was like I needed drugs to function. It was literally like escaping the reality of the pain, but it was not permanent. I was a high-functioning drug addict and I became a master manipulator. During my twenties I had four children. During my thirties I had two more children.

I was able to move through life without committing to my children or the women who had the children because I was numb. My journey to healing included learning how to live with compassion and learning how to communicate so that I could be present for my own life. Today I am very aware that it is important to consistently communicate with love and respect.

During rehab, I had to let them know that I didn't know how to feel. I could not understand how they were able to cry, but I knew that was what I really needed. Sharing my truth about that reality has helped me get to the root of the negative patterns related to generational curses.

Getting to the root of the generational curses helped me gain a new perspective about fatherhood and forgiveness. My dad died with the answers to the questions that I had about my identity and about life.

I wanted him to see me with his attention. I wanted him to see me as his son. I wanted to go for rides in his car. I wanted to go places with him like to the barber shop to get a haircut. I wanted him to coach me through the years that I played sports. I wanted him to give me instructions while I was on the court. I wanted to go out to eat with my father after the game to discuss the game. I wanted my father to see and celebrate me and my accomplishments.

I wanted my father to be present. I wanted my father to hug me. I wanted my father to give me words of affirmation. I did not want to be alone so much. I wanted to be told by my father, "I love you."

I got to the point of being sick and tired of the unknown. I did not have an identity so using drugs was a way to hold on to the people who appeared to have it all together. Trying to find love, identity and belonging is what led to my first crack cocaine use.

PEACE WITH BROKEN PIECES

The person who introduced me to drugs had the "it" factor and always seemed like the center of attention. That person seemed to belong to the in-crowd that had clout and friends. That person knew what to say and how to say it, to get the desired results. Moving through life like that was very attractive to me.

The group was very accepting of all my choices. They were okay with everything that I was confused about. They were giving me information and inspiration, but from the wrong place. I remind the people in my life on a regular basis, "Be aware of where you get your information and inspiration."

That phase of my adult life represented a pattern that was developed during my teen years. My uncle took me to play basketball in other communities. I shared a lot of time with my uncle.

As my uncle was trying to take me out of one world and protect me from one type of lifestyle; the complexity of the world that he lived in seemed attractive because it made me feel good. The life that my father was living surrounded by drugs did not feel good to me. During my teen years about age fifteen or sixteen, I witnessed a lifestyle that was attractive to me because I was surrounded by women.

I felt like I belonged in that circle. The attention and touch of women felt good to me because it was instant gratification. That was around the time that I started wearing a mask to try to blend in with the crowd. People accumulate masks to be accepted and that is exactly what I did. I often wore multiple masks during that phase of my life. My collection of masks included the tough mask, the cool mask, the slick mask and the manipulative mask. I had a different mask for each woman.

PEACE WITH BROKEN PIECES

Although I was in a toxic environment, I finally believed that I was able to fit in and the masks became a regular part of my life. I learned to see what worked, when, where and how. I wore various masks until I was a 45-year-old man.

When I was about seven or eight years old, my mother placed chips and a drink in front of me as I sat at a round table. I did not know at the time, but I was visiting my father in prison. I was very confused by the experience. After my mother passed, I found the letters that my father sent her during that time.

There was no conversation about what happened that led my father to prison. That was another broken piece that created an overcrowded bucket of confusion in my life. That is another reason I chose to carry my father with me through my journey to discover peace.

PEACE WITH BROKEN PIECES

Now I feel good because my healing is also the legacy of my father being redeemed and healed. Daily healing is the decision that I have made for us. The moment that I decided to forgive my dad, I was able to experience true forgiveness and true peace within me.

True transformation in my life happened when I invited my father to heal with me, even after his passing. I have learned that as long as I live, the legacy of my father lives. Now everything that I am, he is through my life. My dad was able to hold his own as it relates to street life. I am dedicated to holding my own as it relates to healing and living a life that honors his legacy.

Now I live in a place of forgiveness for my father that has been forged by compassion. Although I did not understand him as a child, I understand him as a man.

PEACE WITH BROKEN PIECES

I hold on to the memory of the game that my dad attended. I remember the spot where he sat in the audience and the one time that he said, "Good game." My dad even analyzed the game. I was so hurt leading up to that moment that I did not see it at the time. Now I see that game as a victory between me and my father.

PEACE WITH BROKEN PIECES

I am thankful for the gift of overtime because it represents the redeemed life that I get to live in the year 2021 and beyond. I am living in the grace that God provided for me to begin my new life. I have lived long enough to understand that I no longer have to fix all the broken pieces. Grace allows me to live in peace with the broken pieces. The grace of God allows me to live a life where I exude love through my actions.

With all that I have learned about life, I would tell my 11-year-old self, "It's going to be okay because every road to something beautiful doesn't always look beautiful in the beginning. You don't see your metamorphosis now, but you will have a new beginning at the end of a long road in life." My life in overtime is full of gratitude because I enjoy rest now. I believe that I can, I will, I must keep striving and walking into all the fullness of my purpose.

I know that I am loved and love represents hope for life. I encourage every person who reads this book to remember, "It doesn't matter if it is one person or 1,000 people, you are loved." I am thankful for my present life and hopeful for my future. By the time I reach 50 years old I look forward to seeing my family tree. I look forward to witnessing the success of the people I have helped, because it brings me joy to see people thrive.

When I have the opportunity to help, everything that I stand for is in order. It is important for me to have the opportunity to share and to express how much I care. Sharing is a way for me to express love and the deep level of gratitude that I have for all that I have lived through. I survived sleeping on benches and receiving rescue mission meals. I did not have gratitude in addiction, but I have gratitude now.

PEACE WITH BROKEN PIECES

The strength that I discovered after surviving my rock bottom, became my foundation. That is why I remind myself daily, my life can only go up from here. I am now on the journey to rebuilding relationships with my children. I constantly remind myself to be humble and patient with my children. Just because I have chosen recovery, it does not mean that my children will recover at the same pace as me.

I understand that my children deserve grace in the process. It is estimated that friends and family members may recover three times slower than the person who was addicted to drugs. I am thankful that my children are starting to see me differently now that I have set boundaries in my life. I was previously a yes man, now I have different responses. Previously I responded with money or chaos. Now I am taking the time to think through decisions and then respond with wisdom.

PEACE WITH BROKEN PIECES

The experience that I enjoy most about being a father is seeing their looks. I am proud of who my children are and all the lessons that I have learned in life. My new reality is now an adjustment for my children.

After all that I have experienced in life, it is worth it if my children learn from me without having to make the same mistakes as me. I want them to learn that choices lead to consequences and what you put into life is what you get out of life.

It is important to believe. It is important to make your next move the right move. I want them to understand that a series of right choices can lead to good outcomes. I apologize to my children for the mistakes that I have made in the past. I live with a dedication to be better for myself and for them, as we look forward to a brighter future.

"PRAY FOR YOUR PART."

"I firmly believe that once you have been rescued, you must join the rescue. I plan to do my part to rescue as many people as possible, for the rest of my life."

POST

Game

PEACE WITH BROKEN PIECES

The game that I played with drugs and addiction has ended. My life after rehab is mainly about living with a renewed sense of peace and purpose. I begin each day with the process of surrender. I have made the conscious decision to be done playing games with my life because I have discovered personal peace and my true worth.

On my journey to discover my personal peace with the broken pieces of my life, I learned that the process of surrender looks different for each person. As a result, I practice the process of surrender by living each day in deep gratitude for all the grace God has given me. I also practice the process of surrender by taking full responsibility for my actions and understanding that I am forgiven.

The process of surrender includes living with a legacy-driven mindset. I want my legacy to be memorable; therefore, I invest the time to think before I act.

PEACE WITH BROKEN PIECES

I want my family to remember me for laying the foundation for what they stand on, even after I am gone. I want them to know this foundation was built on faith, surrender, resilience, perseverance, love, joy and peace! I want to be remembered by my family for breaking the generational curse so they can enjoy freedom. I firmly believe that once you have been rescued, you must join the rescue. I plan to do my part to rescue as many people as possible, for the rest of my life.

I surrender to God every morning because I am willing to live in peace each day. In the past, I was not at peace because I thought everything required a resolution and I needed to win arguments. Now I am at peace in life, even without the answers to every question. I am enjoying my peace. I still live with remnants of that child who grew up not being hugged or loved by his father, but I chose forgiveness because it supports my lifestyle of peace.

PEACE WITH BROKEN PIECES

The process of surrender also includes me investing time to express my gratitude for redemption. In my life, redemption looks like God. It looks like grace, miracles, victory, love, joy and peace. Redemption also looks like making the daily decision to enjoy the life that I was put here to live. Redemption consists of me investing the effort to make right of my wrongs.

I live with the understanding that even if I can't right every wrong; I can live in peace with broken pieces. I am thankful for redemption because it means that I am blessed to live as the Prince of the King of all creation. I was living a hard life. Now, I truly live the serenity prayer. I surrender everything that I cannot change to God. Fighting looks like trying to go back, but the process of surrender is total freedom to move forward. I understand there are moments that I will go through various phases alone, but I am not just going through for myself.

PEACE WITH BROKEN PIECES

I go through each phase of life to help someone else thrive in life. I live with an awareness that I represent what is possible on the other side of surrender. My dedication to the process of surrender means that I get to rest as it relates to decision making. I am confident in my decisions now. From the age of eleven until forty-five, my life did not feel like rest. Now I understand that rest also means I can freely prioritize and protect my peace. That realization allows me to enjoy the process of surrender without having to fight. I choose to surrender with no regret.

My peace became non-negotiable at the age of 45. I came to know God on a deeper level because drugs did not provide real peace of mind. Someone very close to me died in the midst of their struggle with addiction and I realized that could have been me. Now I recognize God as all divine power. I was led to seek God because I hit rock bottom. I learned that rock bottom was not my destiny.

PEACE WITH BROKEN PIECES

I now understand that sharing my story can help keep the legacy alive of my friend who died from an overdose. I also keep the legacy alive by remaining clean and sober. I keep the legacy alive by reminding people to do as I did on my journey, "Pray for your part."

When God reveals your part to do on earth, I encourage you to get focused on fulfilling your purpose. That is the best way to discover peace, even with broken pieces that may still exist in your life.

Each day that I live to see, I make the decision to believe God. When life seems broken, but you believe God, that can make your life better than it was before. When life seems hopeless, but you believe God, that is your pathway to hope. When you say, "Yes, I believe God" and "Yes, I believe in God," those are two separate realities. I believe God because I have seen the miracle that God created from the mistakes that I made in life.

PEACE WITH BROKEN PIECES

I move at a different pace because I believe God. I can enjoy life, even on the days that I walk slow because I carry a big man. Now I am a Prince of the King of Kings. I roll with love. I give love. I come in peace. I protect my peace because I remember what life was like when I did not have peace. I washed up in a library bathroom for nine months. Now I am fully aware that God has the best for me. What people see as great, good or the best, that is only the beginning. God has so much in store for your life.

The fact that my dad passed while in the midst of addiction, it makes me even more thankful to God for sparing my life. I have a deep level of gratitude to God for allowing me the chance to reflect on my past, evaluate my present, take the lessons that are valuable from my past and leave the pain in the past, as I embrace my future. I am fully aware that not everyone lives through addiction to tell the story of how they survived.

PEACE WITH BROKEN PIECES

There are people who were in the struggle with me who passed in 2021. I am very cognizant of the fact that sharing my story is a way to continue to honor their legacy. During my addiction phase of life, I was an irresponsible father. When I entered their lives again, my daughters were seventeen years old.

I thought money would solve all my problems. Then I used my willingness to pay for everything for my daughters as a tool to control. One of my daughters said, "All you are good for is money." It was a wake-up call for me to enter an addiction treatment center and that place was RCA in St. Charles, Illinois.

God saved me by sending me to the right people and the right place. God made it so clear, now I have no doubt that He is the reason great things happen in my life. The first treatment center that popped up when I searched online was RCA.

PEACE WITH BROKEN PIECES

Initially, I was trying to talk myself out of going before I went, but it was a turning point in my life. It was like I had an appointed time to begin my new life because I was sick and tired of being sick and tired. It was very significant to enter rehab in September of 2021. Picking up the telephone to dial the phone number for rehab was like an out-of-body experience.

There were a lot of hoops that I had to jump through to get into rehab. It was also very expensive to get into rehab. However, I am thankful that I persevered through the process. Now I have a coin that I carry with me each day, which was given to me as a gift, it truly defines my new life. The coin reads, "This day my new life began."

Therapy helped me because it gave me a safe place to start my journey. Before I started therapy I thought, "It's easy for them to say." I didn't believe people could actually relate to me.

PEACE WITH BROKEN PIECES

However, my transformation happened at RCA because everyone that worked with me was an ex-addict. Their words of wisdom and strategies made such a profound impact in my life because I could relate to them, and I learned they could relate to me. I have discovered that even while experiencing broken pieces God created me to be a masterpiece. I have learned that once you master peace, you can see yourself as a true masterpiece. I have rediscovered the gifts that I was born with now that I can see my life more clearly.

I was always very social and friendly. Now I use those gifts to spread light everywhere I go in life. My daily prayer became, "Father God, I surrender to you. Let your will be done." I have learned that it is possible to still have peace, even with the pieces that are broken.

PEACE WITH BROKEN PIECES

While some people may think all the broken pieces have to be reassembled in order to have peace, I have learned how to have peace with the broken pieces. Each broken piece served a purpose and now I refuse to be defined by the broken pieces. My life is defined by the purpose that I have discovered through understanding that I can have peace, even with the broken pieces.

Today, the love that I have for my children motivates me to be better for them. I want to protect them. I want them to have certainty. I want them to know it's okay to express your feelings and seek guidance when you need guidance. I want them to know it's okay to ask for help when you don't feel like you are okay, and you can still be respected. I want them to be confident. I want them to be clear about their identity when they leave out and interact with people each day.

I want them to be aware that they are loved, so they don't seek love in the wrong places. I want them to be strong enough to stand out instead of blending in with a crowd of people who make negative decisions. I want my sons to be the true definition of men. I want my daughters to be the true definition of the strongest parts of my mother; loving, caring, intelligent and willing to sacrifice for the greater good of her children.

I am the father now, that I wish I could have been in 1996. Today I am present. I am thankful that I get the opportunity to hug my children and to tell them, "I love you." I show my sons by example, how to treat a woman. We open doors and hold chairs. I live to show consideration and kindness by example. I want to obliterate phrases that are negatively directed toward women; specifically, when I hear people say, "Women should do certain things." I want to show that women should be cherished and respected.

I also see family with a new perspective. Family is important to me. Family is where you gain the wisdom to get ready for life. Family is also complex. Family is the place where I cultivate unconditional love. Family is forever.

Love is forever. Joy is forever. Peace is forever. While the broken pieces in my life did not go away and the pieces were not reassembled; I made the decision to redefine my life. Now I choose to live each day in "PEACE WITH BROKEN PIECES."

PEACE WITH BROKEN PIECES

Donte' Richards

About the Author

Donte' Richards is a well-educated, truly liberated, man on a mission. This book serves as a definitive, courageous chronicle of his journey from being homeless, sleeping on benches, receiving rescue mission meals, washing up in library bathrooms or men's shelters, to his life today. He traveled a rough journey to discover the true peace that belonged to him. That is why he is dedicated to being non-negotiable about peace.

As the son of a teacher, he learned early in life that education is important. He also learned that teamwork makes the dream work. However, when his support team in life changed, he discovered the resilience to build a new team and redefine his life.

He now invests his time reaching out to help people discover the true peace that leads to an abundant life. He utilizes the lessons that were learned from his past to teach the life lessons necessary to build a brighter future. He is on a path that is being propelled by quantum progress as he achieves each goal. The life lessons that his ancestors taught him has equipped him to make the best out of every opportunity that he receives.

Donte' Richards courageously tells his truth. He shares the details about the good, the challenges, the dark days and the not so beautiful aspects of life. His goal is to help someone else who may be on the journey that he once traveled. His resilience shines through the pain with each word that he has written to uncover the truth that made him free. He has done the inside work and now he is on a mission to be present and encourage you to pray for your part, so that you can surrender with no regret.

PEACE WITH BROKEN PIECES

May the life of Donte' Richards serve as proof that you have the strength to grow from surviving to thriving.

May this book serve as the catalyst to help you discover an abundant life where you can consistently enjoy, "PEACE WITH BROKEN PIECES."

www.ingramcontent.com/pod-product-compliance
Lightning Source LLC
Chambersburg PA
CBHW071224160426
43196CB00012B/2407